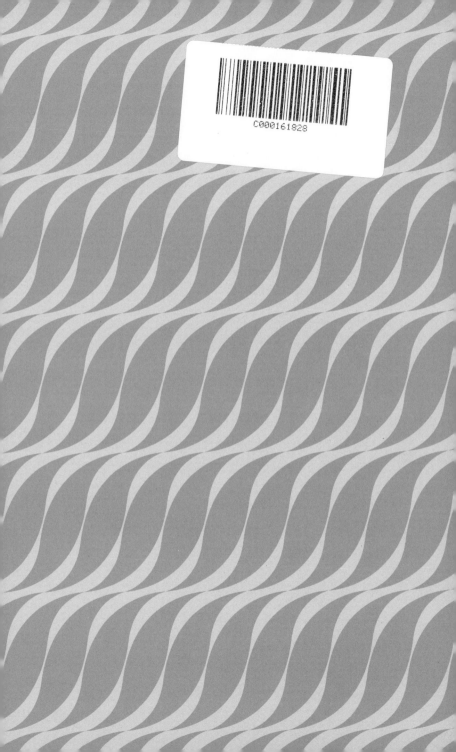

# BEST OF FRANCE

Consultant Editor:
Valerie Ferguson

southwater

# Contents

# Introduction

The cuisine of France is deservedly
admired the world over. What makes it
so special is French people's attitude to
food. They take great pride in the skills
of their chefs, bakers, cheesemakers
and winemakers and have a real
reverence for good basic ingredients,
taking trouble to seek out the freshest
and best-quality basic foods. France is
known for its haute cuisine – elaborate
recipes prepared by skilful chefs in top
restaurants – but more representative
of the country's gastronomy is
traditional home cooking, which tends
to be simple but makes superb use of
the finest seasonal ingredients.

This book celebrates the best of
traditional home cooking with classic
recipes from all over the country.
There are timeless soups and starters,
such as Vichysoisse and Tapenade with
Quails' Eggs; fish and seafood dishes
like Bouillabaisse and Mouclade;
chicken and meat dishes such as Coq
au Vin and Toulouse Cassoulet; and
vegetarian specialities like Ratatouille
and Omelette with Herbs. Tarte Tatin
and Crêpes Suzette with Cointreau are
among the luscious desserts.

As these step-by-step recipes prove,
you certainly do not have to live in
France to enjoy cooking and eating
the French way.

# Ingredients

The key words are "fresh" and "top-quality" when it comes to selecting ingredients for French cooking at home.

## Fish & Seafood

The firm, white, meaty flesh of monkfish holds its shape well during cooking.

A small, round fish with a rosy-pink skin, red mullet is often grilled or baked whole.

*Red mullet*

The firm, pink, superbly flavoured flesh of salmon suits most cooking methods.

A highly esteemed flat fish, turbot has a tasty, white flesh that may be steamed, fried or grilled.

Very versatile, mild-flavoured shellfish, prawns combine well with many other kinds of fish, and are generally used in Bouillabaisse.

Available all year round, mussels have a wonderful, sweet flavour.

The sweet-tasting, meaty shellfish, scallops are the stars of Coquilles St Jacques.

*Mussels*

## Chicken & Meat

Popular for many French dishes is the young and tender cornfed roasting chicken used in Coq au Vin.

The French use various cooking methods for beef, depending on the

*Cornfed chicken*

cut, but one of the best-known is the *daube*, in which it is braised slowly in the oven with wine and herbs.

The leg and best end of neck *(carré)* of lamb are enjoyed roasted, often with pulses such as haricot beans or Puy lentils.

Fresh (as opposed to cured), succulent pork combines wonderfully with products from Normandy, such as

*Puy lentils*

cream, apples and Calvados, and also makes delicious pâtés.

Made from coarsely cut, fresh pork, Toulouse sausages are used in cassoulets, but can also be simply fried or grilled.

## Dairy Products

French cooking makes generous use of milk, butter, cream and crème fraîche. They give a rich, creamy texture and flavour to soups, casseroles and desserts.

France is renowned for its vast range of cheeses made from cow's, ewe's and goat's milk.

Eggs are essential for that most versatile of fast foods, the omelette, and the soufflé.

*Cheeses*

# Vegetables & Salads

Enjoyed as a delicately flavoured vegetable in their own right, courgettes are also an ingredient in the classic vegetable stew, Ratatouille.

A crisp, aniseed-flavoured, bulb-like vegetable, fennel goes well with fish.    *Fennel*

Resembling a large thistle head, the bottom part of the globe artichoke's leaves and the tender heart are edible, but the hairy "choke" is discarded.

Black olives are used frequently in southern French cooking for stuffings, sauces, stews and the pâté known as Tapenade.

The vegetables that can be relied upon to bring flavour to any savoury dish are onions, shallots and leeks.

*Black olives*

Fresh-flavoured green pepper is sweeter when red, yellow and orange. Peppers are an essential ingredient of Ratatouille.    *Onions*

Versatile, delicious and colourful, ripe tomatoes are used in salads and cooked dishes.

With their rich, earthy flavour, wild    *Tomatoes*
mushrooms are used extensively. The most prized are chanterelles, morels and ceps. All kinds of salad leaves are used, from sweet to bitter.    *Ceps*

# Fruit

Grown in abundance, apples are used in both savoury and sweet dishes.

Used in the classic baked dessert, Clafoutis, black cherries are delicious.

Enjoyed in the summer, raspberries, strawberries and blueberries are often eaten in chilled desserts. Citrus fruit, such as oranges and lemons, feature in savoury and sweet dishes. Oranges    *Black cherries*
are a key ingredient of the spectacular flambéed dessert Crêpes Suzette with Cointreau, ideal for a special occasion.

*Raspberries*

# Herbs & Aromatics

French cuisine makes copious use of fresh green herbs, including parsley, basil, dill, thyme, sorrel, marjoram, bay, chervil, tarragon and chives.

Saffron is used in fish dishes like Bouillabaisse and Mouclade. Quatre épices (a mixture of    *Thyme*
ground cloves, cinnamon, nutmeg and pepper) gives a lift to meat pâtés.

# Flavourings & Chocolate

Generous use is made of red and white wine in savoury and sweet dishes, while liqueurs such as pastis, Calvados and framboise make desserts even more irresistible.

Red and white wine vinegars are used for savoury dishes and salads.

The best-quality dark or white chocolate makes sumptuous desserts.

# Stocks

To achieve the best results with the recipes in this book you will need good-quality home-made stock.

## Fish Stock
Makes about 1.75 litres/
3 pints/7½ cups

INGREDIENTS
1 onion
1 carrot
1 celery stick
fish bones, skin and trimmings
6 black peppercorns
2 bay leaves
3 fresh parsley sprigs

**1** Peel and coarsely slice the onion. Peel and chop the carrot, and scrub and slice the celery.

**2** Place the prepared vegetables with all the other ingredients in a large saucepan and add 1.75 litres/3 pints/ 7½ cups water to cover. Bring to the boil, skim the surface and simmer, uncovered, for 20 minutes. Strain.

**3** Store for up to 4 days in the fridge or several months in the freezer.

## Brown Stock
Makes about 1.75 litres/
3 pints/7½ cups

INGREDIENTS
30 ml/2 tbsp vegetable oil
675 g/1½ lb shin of beef, untrimmed
    and cut into pieces
1 bouquet garni
2 onions, trimmed and quartered
2 carrots, trimmed and chopped
2 celery sticks, sliced
5 ml/1 tsp black peppercorns
2.5 ml/½ tsp salt

**1** Preheat the oven to 220°C/425°F Gas 7. Drizzle the vegetable oil over the bottom of a roasting tin and then add the meat. Coat in the oil and bake for 25–30 minutes, or until well browned, turning regularly to ensure even browning.

**2** Transfer the meat to a large saucepan, add the remaining ingredients and cover with 3.2 litres/5½ pints/ 14 cups water. Bring to the boil, skim the surface, then partially cover and simmer for 2½–3 hours, or until reduced to 1.75 litres/3 pints/7½ cups.

**3** Strain the stock and allow to cool; remove the solidified fat before use. Store for up to 4 days in the fridge or several months in the freezer.

## Chicken or White Stock

Makes about 1.5 litres/
2½ pints/6¼ cups

INGREDIENTS

1 onion
4 cloves
1 carrot
2 leeks
2 celery sticks
1 cooked or raw chicken carcass or
    675 g/1½ lb veal bones, cut into pieces
1 bouquet garni
8 black peppercorns
2.5 ml/½ tsp salt

**1** Peel the onion, cut into quarters and spike each quarter with a clove. Scrub and roughly chop the remaining vegetables. Place all the vegetables in a large saucepan with the rest of the stock ingredients.

**2** Cover with 1.75 litres/3 pints/ 7½ cups water. Bring to the boil, skim the surface and simmer, partially covered, for 2 hours. Strain and allow to cool. When cold, remove the hardened fat before using. Store for up to 4 days in the fridge or several months in the freezer.

# Glossary of Terms

**Bake Blind:** to bake or partially bake a pastry case to prevent it becoming soggy when a filling is added.

**Beurre Manié:** equal parts of butter and flour blended to a paste and whisked into simmering cooking liquid for thickening.

**Bouquet Garni:** a bunch of herbs, usually including a bay leaf, thyme sprigs and parsley stalks, used to impart flavour during cooking, often tied for easy removal.

**Croûtons:** small crisp pieces of fried or baked crustless bread.

**Fold:** to combine ingredients, using a large rubber spatula or metal spoon, by cutting down through the centre of the bowl, then along the side and up to the top in a semicircular motion; it is important not to deflate or overwork ingredients while folding.

**Gratiné:** a browned, crisp surface to a baked dish.

**Herbes de Provence:** a mixture of aromatic dried herbs, which grow wild in Provence, usually thyme, marjoram, oregano and summer savory.

**Julienne:** thin matchstick pieces of vegetables, fruit or other food.

**Papillote:** a greased non-stick baking paper or foil parcel, traditionally heart-shaped, enclosing food for cooking.

**Simmer:** to keep a liquid at below boiling point so that it just trembles.

**Skim:** to remove froth or scum from the surface of stocks, etc.

# Vichyssoise

This classic chilled soup was named after its inventor's home town of Vichy.

Serves 4–6

INGREDIENTS
50 g/2 oz/¼ cup unsalted butter
450 g/1 lb leeks, white parts only, thinly sliced
3 large shallots, diced
250 g/9 oz floury potatoes, diced
1 litre/1¾ pints/4 cups light chicken stock
  or water
300 ml/½ pint/1¼ cups double cream
iced water (optional)
a little lemon juice (optional)
salt and freshly ground black pepper
snipped fresh chives, to garnish

**1** Melt the butter in a heavy-based saucepan and cook the leeks and shallots gently, covered, for 15–20 minutes until soft but not browned. Add the potatoes and cook, uncovered, for a few minutes.

**2** Stir in the stock, 5ml/1 tsp salt and pepper to taste. Bring to the boil, then simmer, partly covered, for 15 minutes or until the potatoes are soft.

**3** Cool, then process until smooth in a blender or food processor. Sieve into a bowl and stir in the cream. Taste and adjust the seasoning as necessary. Add a little iced water if the consistency seems too thick.

**4** Chill the soup for at least 4 hours or until very cold. Taste for seasoning and add a squeeze of lemon juice if required. Pour into bowls, sprinkle with chives and serve immediately.

VARIATION: This soup can also be served hot, if you prefer.

# French Onion Soup

In France *Soupe à l'Oignon Gratiné* is popular bistro fare.

Serves 6–8

INGREDIENTS

15 g/½ oz/1 tbsp butter
30 ml/2 tbsp olive oil
4 large onions, about 675 g/1½ lb, thinly sliced
2–4 garlic cloves, finely chopped
5 ml/1 tsp sugar
2.5 ml/½ tsp dried thyme
30 ml/2 tbsp plain flour
120 ml/4 fl oz/½ cup dry white wine
2 litres/3½ pints/8 cups chicken or beef stock
30 ml/2 tbsp brandy (optional)
6–8 stick slices French bread, toasted
1 garlic clove
350 g/12 oz grated Gruyère cheese

**1** In a large, heavy-based saucepan, heat the butter and oil and fry the onions for 10–12 minutes until softened and beginning to brown.

**2** Add the chopped garlic, sugar and thyme and continue cooking for 30–35 minutes, stirring frequently.

**3** Stir in the flour until well blended. Add the wine and stock and bring to the boil. Skim off any foam, then reduce the heat and simmer gently for 45 minutes. Stir in the brandy, if using.

**4** Preheat the grill. Rub each slice of toasted bread with the garlic clove. Place six or eight ovenproof soup bowls on a baking sheet and fill three-quarters full with soup.

**5** Float a piece of toast in each bowl. Top with grated cheese and grill about 15 cm/6 in from the heat for 3–4 minutes until the cheese bubbles. Serve piping hot.

# Pistou

A delicious vegetable soup from Nice in the south of France.

Serves 4–6

INGREDIENTS
1 courgette, diced
1 small potato, diced
1 shallot, chopped
1 carrot, diced
225 g/8 oz can chopped tomatoes
1.2 litres/2 pints/5 cups vegetable stock
50 g/2 oz French beans, cut into
    1 cm/½ in lengths
50 g/2 oz/½ cup frozen petits pois
50 g/2 oz/½ cup small pasta shapes
60–90 ml/4–6 tbsp home-made or
    bought pesto
15 ml/1 tbsp sun-dried tomato paste
salt and freshly ground black pepper
grated Parmesan cheese, to serve

1 Place the courgette, potato, shallot, carrot and tomatoes in a large pan. Add the stock and season with salt and pepper. (If using bought stock, season at the end of cooking.) Bring to the boil, then cover and simmer for 20 minutes.

2 Add the French beans, petits pois and pasta. Cook the soup for a further 10 minutes until the pasta is tender. Adjust the seasoning to taste.

3 Ladle the soup into individual bowls. Mix together the pesto and sun-dried tomato paste, and stir a spoonful into each serving. Serve with grated Parmesan cheese to sprinkle into each bowl.

# Artichokes with Garlic & Herb Butter

What better way to enjoy artichokes than this, as the French do?

Serves 4

INGREDIENTS
2 large or 4 medium globe artichokes
salt

FOR THE GARLIC AND HERB BUTTER
75 g/3 oz/6 tbsp butter
1 garlic clove, crushed
15 ml/1 tbsp chopped mixed fresh tarragon,
    marjoram and parsley

**1** Wash the artichokes well in cold water. Using a sharp knife, cut off the stalks level with the bases. Cut off the top 1 cm/½ in of leaves. Snip off the pointed ends of the remaining leaves with scissors.

**2** Put the prepared artichokes in a large saucepan of lightly salted water. Bring to the boil, cover and cook for about 40–45 minutes or until a lower leaf comes away easily when gently pulled. Remove from the pan and leave upside down to drain thoroughly.

**3** To make the garlic and herb butter, melt the butter over a low heat, add the garlic and cook for 30 seconds. Remove from the heat, stir in the herbs and pour into one or two small serving bowls. Place the artichokes on serving plates and serve with the garlic and herb butter. Some crusty French bread to soak up any butter would also be good.

# Coquilles St Jacques

A classic French starter, that calls for the best-quality scallops possible to ensure a truly wonderful result. You will also need four well scrubbed scallop shells to serve these.

Serves 4

INGREDIENTS
450 g/1 lb potatoes, chopped
50 g/2 oz/¼ cup butter
4 large or 8 small scallops
120 ml/4 fl oz/½ cup fish stock
fresh dill sprigs, to garnish
grilled lemon wedges, to serve

FOR THE SAUCE
25 g/1 oz/2 tbsp butter
25 g/1 oz/¼ cup plain flour
300 ml/½ pint/1¼ cups milk
30 ml/2 tbsp single cream
115 g/4 oz/1 cup grated mature
    Cheddar cheese
salt and freshly ground black pepper

**2** Spoon the mashed potatoes into a piping bag fitted with a star nozzle. Pipe neatly around the outside of four cleaned scallop shells.

**3** Simmer the scallops in a little fish stock for 3 minutes or until just firm. Drain the scallops and slice finely. Set them aside.

**1** Place the chopped potatoes in a large saucepan, cover with water, bring to the boil and cook for 15 minutes or until tender. Drain thoroughly and mash with the butter. Preheat the oven to 200°C/400°F/Gas 6.

**4** To make the sauce, melt the butter in a small saucepan, add the flour and cook over a low heat for a couple of minutes. Gradually add the milk and cream, stirring continuously, and cook until thickened.

**5** Stir in the cheese and cook until melted. Season to taste. Spoon a little sauce in the base of each shell. Divide the scallops among the shells and then pour the remaining sauce over the scallops.

**6** Bake the scallops in the oven for 10 minutes or until golden. Garnish with dill. Serve with grilled lemon wedges.

# Country-style Pâté with Leeks

This traditional French *Pâté de Porc aux Poireaux* uses leeks for a fresher flavour and a lighter-than-usual result.

## Serves 8–10

### INGREDIENTS
15 g/½ oz/1 tbsp butter
450 g/1 lb leeks, white and light green parts, thinly sliced
2 or 3 large garlic cloves, finely chopped
1 kg/2¼ lb lean pork leg or shoulder, cut into 4 cm/1½ in cubes
150 g/5 oz rindless smoked streaky bacon rashers
7.5 ml/1½ tsp chopped fresh thyme
3 fresh sage leaves, finely chopped
1.5 ml/¼ tsp quatre épices (a mix of ground cloves, cinnamon, nutmeg and pepper)
1.5 ml/¼ tsp ground cumin
pinch of grated nutmeg
2.5 ml/½ tsp salt
5 ml/1 tsp freshly ground black pepper
1 bay leaf

**1** Melt the butter in a large, heavy saucepan, add the leeks, cover and cook gently for 10 minutes, stirring occasionally. Add the garlic and continue cooking for about another 10 minutes until the leeks are very soft. Set aside to cool.

> COOK'S TIP: In France, *cornichons* (small dill pickles) and mustard are traditional accompaniments for pork terrines, along with slices of crusty baguette.

**2** Chop the pork to a coarse purée in a food processor. Alternatively, pass it through the coarse blade of a meat mincer. Transfer to a large mixing bowl and remove any white stringy bits. Reserve two of the bacon rashers for garnishing, and chop or mince the remainder. Add the bacon to the pork.

**3** Preheat the oven to 180°C/350°F/ Gas 4. Line the base and sides of a 1.5 litre/2½ pint/6¼ cup terrine or loaf tin with greaseproof paper or non-stick baking paper.

**4** Add the leeks, herbs, spices and salt and pepper to the pork and bacon then, using a wooden spoon or your fingertips, mix until well combined.

**5** Spoon the mixture into the terrine or loaf tin, pressing it down well. Tap firmly to settle the mixture and smooth the top. Arrange the bay leaf and remaining bacon rashers on top, then cover tightly with foil.

6 Place the terrine or tin in a roasting tin and pour in boiling water to come halfway up the sides. Bake for about 1¼ hours.

7 Lift the terrine or tin out of the roasting tin and place in a shallow dish. Put a weighted baking sheet on the pâté while it cools. (Liquid will seep out during this time.) Chill and serve sliced.

# Tapenade with Quails' Eggs

Tapenade is a pâté, made with black olives, from the south of France.

Serves 6

INGREDIENTS
225 g/8 oz/2 cups pitted black olives
2 large garlic cloves, peeled
15 ml/1 tbsp salted capers, rinsed
6 canned or bottled anchovy fillets, drained
50 g/2 oz good-quality canned tuna
5–10 ml/1–2 tsp cognac (optional)
5 ml/1 tsp chopped fresh thyme
30 ml/2 tbsp chopped fresh parsley
30–60 ml/2–4 tbsp extra virgin olive oil
dash of lemon juice
30 ml/2 tbsp crème fraîche or fromage frais
12–18 quails' eggs
freshly ground black pepper
French bread, unsalted butter and sea salt,
   to serve

FOR THE CRUDITÉS
1 bunch spring onions, halved if large
1 bunch radishes, trimmed
1 large fennel bulb, cut into thin wedges

**1** Process the olives, garlic, capers, anchovies and tuna in a food processor or blender until coarse or smooth, according to taste. Blend in the cognac, if using, the herbs and enough olive oil to make a paste. Season to taste with pepper and a dash of lemon juice. Stir in the crème fraîche or fromage frais, and transfer to a serving bowl.

**2** Place the quails' eggs in a saucepan, cover with cold water and bring to the boil. Cook for 2 minutes, then immediately drain and plunge the eggs into iced water to stop them from cooking further and to make them easier to shell.

**3** When the eggs are cold, part-shell them. Arrange the eggs with the tapenade and crudités and serve, offering French bread, unsalted butter and sea salt to accompany them.

# Grilled Goat's Cheese Salad

*Salade de Chèvre,* with tangy goat's cheese, makes a superb French starter.

Serves 4

INGREDIENTS

2 firm round whole goat's cheeses,
    such as *Crottin de Chavignol,*
    about 65–115 g/2½–4 oz each
4 slices French bread
extra virgin olive oil, for drizzling
175 g/6 oz/5–6 cups mixed salad leaves,
    including soft and bitter varieties
snipped fresh chives,
    to garnish

FOR THE VINAIGRETTE DRESSING
½ garlic clove
5 ml/1 tsp Dijon mustard
5 ml/1 tsp white wine vinegar
5 ml/1 tsp dry white wine
45 ml/3 tbsp extra virgin olive oil
salt and freshly ground
    black pepper

**1** To make the dressing, rub a large salad bowl with the cut side of the garlic clove. Combine the mustard, vinegar and wine with salt and pepper in the bowl. Whisk in the oil, 15 ml/ 1 tbsp at a time, to form a thick vinaigrette. Taste for seasoning.

**2** Preheat the grill to hot. Cut the goat's cheeses in half crossways, using a sharp knife. Arrange the bread slices on a baking sheet and toast them on one side. Turn over and place a piece of cheese, cut side up, on each slice. Drizzle with olive oil and grill until the cheese is lightly browned.

**3** Add the leaves to the salad bowl and toss. Divide the salad among four plates, top each with a goat's cheese croûton and serve, garnished with chives.

# Turbot en Papillote

Enjoy this way of cooking fish in a parcel, as they do in France.

Serves 4

INGREDIENTS

2 carrots, cut into thin julienne strips
2 courgettes, cut into thin julienne strips
2 leeks, cut into thin julienne strips
1 fennel bulb, cut into thin julienne strips
2 tomatoes, peeled, seeded and diced
30 ml/2 tbsp chopped fresh dill,
   tarragon, or chervil
4 turbot fillets, about 200 g/7 oz each,
   cut in half
20 ml/4 tsp olive oil
60 ml/4 tbsp white wine or fish stock
salt and freshly ground black pepper
pine nuts, to garnish

**1** Preheat the oven to 190°C/375°F/ Gas 5. Cut four pieces of non-stick baking paper, 45 cm/18 in long. Fold each in half and cut into a heart shape.

**2** Open the paper hearts. Arrange one quarter of each of the vegetables next to the fold of each heart. Sprinkle with salt and pepper and half the chopped herbs. Arrange two pieces of turbot fillet over each bed of vegetables, overlapping the thin end of one piece and the thicker end of the other. Sprinkle over the rest of the herbs, the oil and wine or stock.

**3** Fold the top half of one of the paper hearts over the fish and vegetables and, beginning at the rounded end, fold the edges of the paper over, twisting and folding to form an airtight packet.

**4** Slide the parcels on to baking sheets and bake for about 10 minutes or until the paper is lightly browned and well puffed. Slide each parcel on to a warmed plate and serve.

# Monkfish with Tomatoes

The tasty tomato sauce makes *Lotte à la Provençale* a special dish.

Serves 4

INGREDIENTS
800 g/1¾ lb monkfish tail, skinned
   and filleted
plain flour, for dusting
45–60 ml/3–4 tbsp olive oil
120 ml/4 fl oz/½ cup dry white wine or
   fish stock
3 ripe tomatoes, peeled, seeded
   and chopped
2.5 ml/½ tsp dried thyme
16 black olives (preferably
   Niçoise), pitted
15–30 ml/1–2 tbsp capers,
   rinsed
15 ml/1 tbsp chopped fresh basil
salt and freshly ground
   black pepper
pine nuts, to garnish

**1** Using a thin, sharp knife, remove any membrane from the monkfish tail. Cut the fillets diagonally into 12 slices. Season and dust with flour.

**2** Heat a large, heavy frying pan until very hot. Add the oil and swirl to coat. Add the fish and cook over medium-high heat for 1–2 minutes on each side until lightly browned and the flesh is opaque. Transfer to a warmed plate.

**3** Add the wine or stock to the pan and boil for 1–2 minutes, stirring. Add the tomatoes and thyme and cook for 2 minutes, then stir in the olives, capers and basil. Cook for a minute. Divide the fish among four warmed plates. Spoon over the sauce, garnish with pine nuts and serve.

# Grilled Red Mullet with Herbs

This simple dish is a speciality of Provence where local herbs are extensively used in cooking.

Serves 4

INGREDIENTS
olive oil, for brushing
4 red mullet, 225–275 g/8–10 oz each,
  cleaned and scaled
fresh herb sprigs (parsley, dill or thyme)
30–45 ml/2–3 tbsp pastis (anise liqueur)

1 About one hour before cooking, light a charcoal fire: when ready the coals should be grey with no flames. Brush a hinged grilling rack with oil or preheat the grill and oil the rack.

2 Brush each fish with a little olive oil and stuff the cavity with a few herb sprigs. Secure the fish in the grilling rack and grill for 15–20 minutes, turning once, or cook under the grill.

3 Transfer the fish to a warmed, flameproof serving dish. Pour the pastis into a small saucepan and heat for a moment or two, then tilt the pan and carefully ignite with a long match. Pour evenly over the fish and serve.

*Right: Grilled Red Mullet with Herbs (top); Salmon Steaks with Sorrel Sauce*

# Salmon Steaks with Sorrel Sauce

*Saumon à l'Oseille* is a traditional dish that makes the most of the slightly bitter taste of the herb sorrel.

Serves 2

INGREDIENTS
15 g/½ oz/1 tbsp butter
2 shallots, finely chopped
45 ml/3 tbsp whipping cream
90 g/3½ oz fresh sorrel leaves
2 salmon steaks, about 250 g/9 oz each
5 ml/1 tsp olive oil
salt and freshly ground black pepper
fresh sage, to garnish

1 In a small saucepan, melt the butter over a medium heat and fry the shallots, stirring frequently, until just softened. Add the cream and sorrel and cook until the sorrel is completely wilted, stirring constantly.

2 Meanwhile, season the salmon steaks with salt and pepper. Brush a non-stick frying pan with the oil and place over a medium heat until hot. Add the salmon steaks and cook for about 5 minutes, turning once, until the flesh is opaque next to the bone.

3 Arrange the salmon steaks on two warmed plates and pour the sorrel sauce over them. Garnish with sage and serve.

# Bouillabaisse

Different variations of this fish stew abound along the Mediterranean coast.

Serves 8

INGREDIENTS

2.5 kg/5½ lb white fish, such as sea bass,
    snapper or monkfish, filleted and skinned
45 ml/3 tbsp extra virgin olive oil
grated rind of 1 orange
1 garlic clove, very finely chopped
pinch of saffron strands
30 ml/2 tbsp pastis (anise liqueur)
1 small fennel bulb, finely chopped
1 large onion, finely chopped
225 g/8 oz small new potatoes, sliced
900 g/2 lb large raw Mediterranean prawns,
    peeled (retain the head and shells)
croûtons, to serve

FOR THE STOCK

30 ml/2 tbsp olive oil
2 leeks, sliced
1 onion, halved and sliced
1 red pepper, seeded and sliced
1–1.3 kg/2¼–3 lb fish heads, bones
    and trimmings
675 g/1½ lb ripe tomatoes, seeded
4 garlic cloves, sliced
1 bouquet garni
thinly pared rind of ½ orange
2 or 3 pinches saffron strands

FOR THE *ROUILLE*

25 g/1 oz/½ cup soft white breadcrumbs
1–2 garlic cloves, very finely chopped
½ red pepper, roasted
5 ml/1 tsp tomato paste
120 ml/4 fl oz/½ cup extra virgin olive oil

**1** Cut the fish fillets into serving pieces, then trim off any thin parts and reserve for the stock. Put the fish in a bowl with 30 ml/2 tbsp of the olive oil, the grated orange rind, garlic, saffron and pastis (anise liqueur). Turn to coat well, cover and chill.

**2** For the stock, heat the oil in a large saucepan. Add the leeks, onion and red pepper and cook over a medium heat for about 5 minutes until the onion starts to soften. Add the fish heads, bones and trimmings, with any heads or shells from the prawns. Then add the remaining ingredients and enough cold water to cover by 2.5 cm/1 in.

**3** Bring to the boil, skim off any foam that rises to the surface, then simmer, covered, for 30 minutes, skimming once or twice more. Strain.

**4** To make the *rouille,* soak the breadcrumbs in water, then squeeze dry. Put the breadcrumbs in a food processor with the garlic, roasted red pepper and tomato paste and process until smooth. With the machine running, slowly pour the oil through the feed tube, scraping down the sides once or twice.

**5** To finish the bouillabaisse, heat the remaining 15 ml/1 tbsp olive oil in a wide flameproof casserole over a medium heat.

**6** Cook the fennel and onion for about 5 minutes, then add the stock. Bring to the boil, add the potatoes and cook for 5–7 minutes. Reduce the heat to medium and add the fish, starting with the thickest pieces and adding the thinner ones after 2 or 3 minutes. Add the prawns and simmer gently until all the fish and shellfish are cooked.

**7** Transfer the fish, shellfish and potatoes to a heated tureen or individual soup plates. Adjust the seasoning and ladle the soup over. Serve with croûtons spread with *rouille*.

# Mouclade

This is a traditional dish of mussels cooked with shallots, garlic and saffron from the west Atlantic coast of France, which looks as superb as it tastes.

Serves 6

INGREDIENTS

2 kg/4½ lb fresh mussels, scrubbed and
    beards removed
250 g/9 oz shallots, finely chopped
300 ml/½ pint/1¼ cups medium white wine,
    such as Vouvray
generous pinch of saffron strands
    (about 12 strands)
50 g/2 oz/¼ cup butter
2 celery sticks, finely chopped
5 ml/1 tsp fennel seeds, lightly crushed
2 large garlic cloves, finely chopped
250 ml/8 fl oz/1 cup fish or
    vegetable stock
1 bay leaf
pinch of cayenne pepper
2 large egg yolks
150 ml/¼ pint/⅔ cup double cream
juice of ½–1 lemon
30–45 ml/2–3 tbsp chopped
    fresh parsley
salt and freshly ground black pepper

**1** Discard any mussels that do not shut when tapped sharply. Place 30 ml/2 tbsp of the shallots in a wide saucepan with the wine and bring to the boil. Add half the mussels and cover, then boil rapidly for 1 minute, shaking the pan once. Remove all the mussels, discarding any that remain closed. Repeat with the remaining mussels.

**2** Remove the top half-shell from all the mussels. Strain the cooking liquid through a fine sieve into a bowl and stir in the saffron, then set aside.

**3** Melt the butter in a heavy-based saucepan. Add the remaining shallots and the chopped celery and cook over a low heat, stirring occasionally, for 5–6 minutes until softened but not browned. Add the fennel seeds and half of the garlic, then cook for another 2–3 minutes.

**4** Pour in the reserved mussel liquid, bring to the boil and simmer for 5 minutes before adding the stock, bay leaf and cayenne. Season with salt and pepper to taste, then simmer, uncovered, for 5–10 minutes.

**5** Beat the egg yolks with the cream, then whisk in a ladleful of the hot liquid followed by the juice of half a lemon. Whisk this mixture back into the sauce.

6 Cook the sauce over a very low heat, without allowing it to boil, for 5–10 minutes until slightly thickened. Stir from time to time. Taste for seasoning and add more lemon juice if necessary.

7 Mix the remaining garlic and most of the parsley into the sauce with the mussels and reheat for 1 minute. Distribute the mussels among six soup plates and ladle the sauce over. Sprinkle with parsley and serve.

# Roast Chicken with Lemon & Herbs

In France the evocative sight and smell of chicken roasting on the spit – *Poulet Rôti* – can often be found in *charcuteries*. This version, with its fragrant stuffing, tastes just as good.

Serves 4

INGREDIENTS
1.3 kg/3 lb chicken
1 unwaxed lemon, halved
1 small bunch fresh thyme sprigs
1 bay leaf
15 g/½ oz/1 tbsp butter, softened
60–90 ml/4–6 tbsp chicken
   stock or water
salt and freshly ground
   black pepper

**1** Preheat the oven to 200°C/400°F/ Gas 6. Season the chicken inside and out with salt and pepper.

**2** Squeeze the juice of one lemon half and then place the juice, the squeezed lemon half, the thyme and bay leaf in the chicken cavity. Tie the legs with string and rub the breast with butter.

**3** Place the chicken on a rack in a roasting tin. Squeeze over the juice of the other lemon half. Roast the chicken for 1 hour, basting two or three times, or until the juices run clear when the thickest part of the thigh is pierced with a knife.

**4** Pour the juices from the cavity into the roasting tin and transfer the chicken to a carving board. Cover loosely with foil and leave to stand for 10–15 minutes before beginning to carve the chicken.

**5** Skim off the fat from the cooking juices. (A very easy way to do this is by laying sheets of kitchen paper on top. It will absorb the fat.) Add the stock or water and boil over a medium heat, stirring and scraping the base of the pan, until slightly reduced. Strain and serve with the chicken.

# Coq au Vin

This French country casserole was traditionally made with a boiling bird, but these are no longer readily available, so now we use roasting birds.

Serves 6

INGREDIENTS
45 ml/3 tbsp light olive oil
12 shallots
225 g/8 oz rindless streaky bacon
   rashers, chopped
3 garlic cloves, finely chopped
225 g/8 oz small mushrooms, halved
6 boneless chicken thighs
3 boneless chicken breasts, halved
1 bottle red wine
salt and freshly ground
   black pepper
45 ml/3 tbsp chopped fresh parsley,
   to garnish
boiled potatoes, to serve

FOR THE BOUQUET GARNI
3 sprigs each fresh parsley, thyme
   and sage
1 bay leaf
4 peppercorns

FOR THE BEURRE MANIÉ
25 g/1 oz/2 tbsp butter, softened
25 g/1 oz/¼ cup plain flour

**1** Heat the olive oil in a large, flameproof casserole and cook the shallots for 5 minutes or until they are golden. Increase the heat, add the bacon, garlic and halved mushrooms and cook for a further 10 minutes, stirring frequently.

**2** Use a draining spoon to transfer the cooked ingredients to a plate, then brown the chicken portions in the oil remaining in the pan, turning them until they are golden brown all over. Return the shallots, garlic, mushrooms and bacon to the casserole and pour in the red wine.

**3** To make the bouquet garni, tie the ingredients in a bundle in a small piece of muslin and add to the casserole. Bring to the boil, reduce the heat and cover the casserole, then simmer for 30–40 minutes.

**4** To make the beurre manié, cream the butter and flour together in a small bowl, using your fingers or a spoon, to make a smooth paste.

**5** Add small lumps of this paste to the bubbling casserole, stirring well until each piece has melted into the liquid before adding the next. When all the paste has been added, bring back to the boil and simmer for 5 minutes.

**6** Season the casserole to taste with salt and pepper and serve garnished with chopped fresh parsley and accompanied by boiled potatoes.

COOK'S TIP: If there is time, marinate the chicken portions in the wine and bouquet garni for a few hours. This improves the taste and colour. Dry well before frying.

# Roast Leg of Lamb with Beans

In France the shank bone of *Gigot d'Agneau* is not removed, but it is cut through for easier handling. The roast is often served with haricot or flageolet beans, which is typical of the region of Brittany.

Serves 8–10

INGREDIENTS
2.75–3 kg/6–7 lb leg of lamb
3–4 garlic cloves
olive oil
fresh or dried rosemary leaves
450 g/1 lb/2½ cups dried haricot or flageolet
    beans, soaked overnight in cold water
1 bay leaf
30 ml/2 tbsp red wine
150 ml/¼ pint/⅔ cup lamb or beef stock
25 g/1 oz/2 tbsp butter
salt and freshly ground black pepper
watercress, to garnish

**1** Preheat the oven to 220°C/425°F/
Gas 7. Wipe the leg of lamb with damp
kitchen paper and dry the fat covering
well. Cut two or three of the garlic
cloves into 10–12 slivers, then, with the
tip of a knife, cut 10–12 slits into the
lamb and insert the slivers into the slits.
Rub with oil, season with salt and
pepper and sprinkle with rosemary.

**2** Set the lamb on a rack in a shallow
roasting tin and place in the oven.
After 15 minutes, reduce the heat to
180°C/350°F/Gas 4 and continue
to roast for 1½–1¾ hours (about
18 minutes per 450 g/1 lb) or until
a meat thermometer inserted into
the thickest part of the meat registers
57–60°C/135–140°F for medium-rare
to medium meat or 66°C/150°F for
well-done.

**3** Meanwhile, drain the beans and put
in a saucepan with enough fresh water
to cover generously. Add the remaining
garlic and the bay leaf, then bring to
the boil. Reduce the heat and simmer
for 45 minutes–1 hour or until tender.

**4** Transfer the roast to a board and
allow to stand, loosely covered, for
10–15 minutes. Skim off the fat from
the cooking juices, then add the wine
and stock to the tin. Boil over a
medium heat, stirring and scraping the
base of the tin, until slightly reduced.
Strain into a warmed gravy boat.

COOK'S TIP: The quality and age
of dried beans varies; the older they
are the longer they take to cook. For
this reason it is best to cook them
in advance and reheat.

**5** Drain the beans, discard the bay leaf, then toss the beans with the butter until it melts and season with salt and pepper. Garnish the lamb with watercress and serve with the beans and the gravy.

# Herb-crusted Rack of Lamb with Puy Lentils

*Carré d'Agneau* is a delicious roast, ideal for entertaining French-style.

## Serves 4

### INGREDIENTS
2 x 6-bone racks of lamb, chined
50 g/2 oz/1 cup fresh white breadcrumbs
2 large garlic cloves, crushed
90 ml/6 tbsp chopped fresh mixed herbs,
    such as rosemary, thyme, flat leaf parsley
    and marjoram, plus extra whole sprigs
    to garnish
50 g/2 oz/¼ cup butter, melted
salt and freshly ground black pepper
boiled new potatoes, to serve

### FOR THE PUY LENTILS
1 red onion, chopped
30 ml/2 tbsp olive oil
400 g/14 oz can Puy or green lentils, rinsed
    and drained
400 g/14 oz can chopped tomatoes
30 ml/2 tbsp chopped fresh parsley

**1** Preheat the oven to 220°C/425°F/ Gas 7. Trim any excess fat from the lamb, season and place in a roasting tin.

**2** Mix together the breadcrumbs, garlic, chopped herbs and butter. Press the mixture on to the fat side of the lamb. Roast for 25 minutes. Cover with foil and stand for 5 minutes before carving.

**3** To prepare the lentils, cook the onion in the olive oil until softened. Add the lentils and tomatoes and cook gently for 5 minutes, or until the lentils are piping hot. Stir in the parsley and season to taste.

**4** Cut each rack of lamb in half and serve with the lentils and new potatoes. Garnish with herb sprigs.

# Noisettes of Pork with Creamy Calvados & Apple Sauce

This dish makes the most of the sumptuous produce of Normandy.

Serves 4

INGREDIENTS

30 ml/2 tbsp plain flour
4 noisettes of pork, about 175 g/6 oz each,
    firmly tied
25 g/1 oz/2 tbsp butter
4 baby leeks, finely sliced
5 ml/1 tsp mustard seeds, coarsely crushed
30 ml/2 tbsp Calvados (apple brandy)
150 ml/¼ pint/⅔ cup dry white wine
2 Golden Delicious apples, peeled, cored
    and sliced
150 ml/¼ pint/⅔ cup double cream
30 ml/2 tbsp chopped fresh parsley
salt and freshly ground black pepper

**1** Place the flour in a bowl and add plenty of seasoning. Turn the noisettes in the flour mixture to coat lightly.

**2** Melt the butter in a heavy-based frying pan and cook the noisettes until golden on both sides. Remove from the pan and set aside.

**3** Add the leeks to the fat remaining in the pan and cook for 5 minutes. Stir in the mustard seeds and pour in the Calvados, then carefully ignite to burn off the alcohol. When the flames have died down, pour in the wine and replace the pork. Cook gently for 10 minutes, turning the pork frequently.

**4** Add the sliced apples and double cream and simmer for 5 minutes, or until the apples are tender and the sauce is thick, rich and creamy. Taste for seasoning, then stir in the chopped parsley and serve at once.

35

# Toulouse Cassoulet

There are many versions of this regional speciality in south-west France, and it is one of the most famous recipes of traditional home cooking.

Serves 6–8

INGREDIENTS

450 g/1 lb/2½ cups dried white beans
   (haricot or cannellini), soaked overnight in
   cold water, then rinsed and drained
675 g/1½ lb Toulouse sausages
500 g/1¼ lb each boneless lamb and pork
   shoulder, cut into 5 cm/2 in pieces
1 large onion, finely chopped
3–4 garlic cloves, very finely chopped
4 tomatoes, peeled, seeded and chopped
300 ml/½ pint/1¼ cups chicken stock
1 bouquet garni
60 ml/4 tbsp fresh breadcrumbs
salt and freshly ground black pepper

**1** Put the beans in a saucepan with water to cover. Boil vigorously for 10 minutes and drain, then return to a clean saucepan, cover with water and bring to the boil. Reduce the heat and simmer for 45 minutes or until tender, then add a little salt and leave to soak in the cooking water.

**2** Preheat the oven to 180°C/350°F/Gas 4. Prick the sausages, place them in a large, heavy-based frying pan over a medium heat and cook for 20–25 minutes until browned, turning occasionally to brown evenly. Drain on kitchen paper and pour off all but 15 ml/1 tbsp of the fat given off by the sausages from the pan.

**3** Increase the heat to medium-high. Season the lamb and pork and add enough of the meat to the pan to fit easily in one layer. Cook until browned, then transfer to a large dish. Continue browning in batches.

**4** Add the onion and garlic to the pan and cook for 3–4 minutes until just soft, stirring. Stir in the tomatoes and cook for 2–3 minutes, then transfer the vegetables to the meat dish. Add the stock and bring to the boil, then skim off the fat.

**5** Spoon one-quarter of the beans into a large casserole, and top with one-third of the sausages, meat and vegetables. Continue layering, ending with a layer of beans. Tuck in the bouquet garni, pour over the stock and top up with enough of the bean cooking liquid to just cover. (When the cassoulet is finally cooked the beans should be creamy and the stock absorbed.)

**6** Cover the casserole and bake for 2 hours (check and add more bean cooking liquid if it seems dry). Uncover, sprinkle over the fresh breadcrumbs and press with the back of a spoon to moisten them. Continue cooking, uncovered, for approximately 20 minutes more until browned.

COOK'S TIP: This is a very substantial dish, perhaps best eaten at lunchtime, and a very good choice for the weekend as it can be made in advance. If you serve something first, it should be very light.

# Provençal Beef & Olive Daube

A daube is a French method of braising meat with wine and herbs. This version from the Nice area also includes black olives and tomatoes.

Serves 6

INGREDIENTS
1.5 kg/3½ lb topside beef
225 g/8 oz lardons, or thick streaky bacon
    cut into strips
225 g/8 oz carrots, sliced
1 bay leaf
1 fresh thyme sprig
2 fresh parsley stalks
3 garlic cloves
225 g/8 oz/2 cups pitted black olives
400 g/14 oz can chopped tomatoes
crusty bread, flageolet beans or pasta,
    to serve

FOR THE MARINADE
120 ml/4 fl oz/½ cup olive oil
1 onion, sliced
4 shallots, sliced
1 celery stick, sliced
1 carrot, sliced
150 ml/¼ pint/⅔ cup red wine
6 black peppercorns
2 garlic cloves, sliced
1 bay leaf
1 fresh thyme sprig
2 fresh parsley stalks
salt

**1** To make the marinade, heat the oil in a large, shallow pan and add the onion, shallots, celery and carrot.

**2** Cook the marinade for 2 minutes, then lower the heat and add the red wine, peppercorns, garlic, bay leaf, thyme and parsley stalks. Season with salt, cover and leave to simmer gently for 15–20 minutes. Set aside.

**3** Place the beef in a large glass or earthenware dish and pour over the cooled marinade. Cover the dish and leave to marinate in a cool place or in the fridge for 12 hours, turning the meat once or twice.

**4** Preheat the oven to 160°C/325°F/ Gas 3. Lift the meat out of the marinade and fit it snugly into an ovenproof casserole. Add the lardons or bacon and carrots, along with the herbs and garlic. Strain in all the marinade. Cover the casserole with a sheet of greaseproof paper, then the lid and cook in the oven for 2½ hours.

**5** Remove the casserole from the oven and stir in the olives and tomatoes. Re-cover the casserole, return to the oven and cook for a further 30 minutes. Serve the meat cut into thick slices, accompanied by crusty bread, beans or pasta.

# Steak Béarnaise

Béarnaise, a creamy egg and butter sauce flavoured with fresh tarragon, is a classic French accompaniment for griddled, grilled or pan-fried steak.

Serves 4

INGREDIENTS
4 sirloin steaks, about 225 g/8 oz
    each, trimmed
15 ml/1 tbsp sunflower oil
    (optional)
salt and freshly ground
    black pepper

FOR THE BÉARNAISE SAUCE
90 ml/6 tbsp white wine vinegar
12 black peppercorns
2 bay leaves
2 shallots, finely chopped
4 fresh tarragon sprigs
4 egg yolks
225 g/8 oz/1 cup unsalted butter, diced,
    at room temperature
30 ml/2 tbsp chopped
    fresh tarragon
freshly ground white pepper

**1** To make the sauce, put the vinegar, peppercorns, bay leaves, shallots and tarragon sprigs in a small saucepan and simmer until reduced to 30 ml/2 tbsp. Strain through a fine sieve.

**2** Beat the egg yolks with salt and freshly ground white pepper in a small, heatproof bowl. Stand the bowl over a saucepan of very gently simmering water, then beat the strained vinegar into the yolks.

**3** Gradually beat in the butter, one piece at a time, allowing each to melt before adding the next. Do not allow the water to heat beyond a gentle simmer or the sauce will overheat and curdle.

**4** Beat in the tarragon and remove the pan from the heat. The sauce should be smooth, thick and glossy. Cover the surface with clear film or dampened greaseproof paper (to prevent a skin forming) and leave over the pan of hot water (still off the heat) to keep hot.

COOK'S TIP: If you are confident about preparing egg and butter sauces, the best method is to reduce the flavoured vinegar before cooking the steak, then finish the sauce while the steak is cooking. This way, the sauce does not have to be kept hot and there is less risk of overheating it or allowing it to become too thick.

**5** Meanwhile, heat a frying pan, griddle or grill until very hot. Lightly oil the pan if necessary and cook the steaks for 2–4 minutes on each side. The cooking time depends on the thickness of the steaks and your own personal taste. As a general guide, 2–4 minutes will give a medium-rare result.

**6** Serve the steaks on warmed plates. Peel the clear film or dampened greaseproof paper off the sauce and stir it lightly, then spoon it over the steaks. Remember that the classic way to serve sauce Béarnaise is tepid rather than hot.

# Classic Cheese Soufflé

A delicate, melt-in-the-mouth cheese soufflé makes one of the most delightful light meals imaginable – yet another classic French dish.

Serves 2–3

INGREDIENTS
50 g/2 oz/¼ cup butter
30–45 ml/2–3 tbsp dried fine breadcrumbs
200 ml/7 fl oz/scant 1 cup milk
30 g/1¼ oz/3 tbsp plain flour
pinch of cayenne pepper
2.5 ml/½ tsp mustard powder
50 g/2 oz/½ cup grated mature Gruyère cheese
25 g/1 oz/⅓ cup grated Parmesan cheese
4 eggs, separated, plus 1 egg white
salt and freshly ground black pepper

**3** Simmer the sauce for a minute or two, then turn off the heat and whisk in all the Gruyère and half of the Parmesan. Cool a little, then beat in the egg yolks. Check the seasoning: it should be well seasoned. Set aside.

**4** Whisk the egg whites in a large grease-free bowl until they form soft, glossy peaks. Do not overbeat or the whites will become grainy and difficult to fold in.

**1** Preheat the oven to 190°C/375°F/ Gas 5. Gently melt 15 ml/1 tbsp of the butter and use to thoroughly grease a 1.2 litre/2 pint/5 cup soufflé dish. Coat the inside of the dish with breadcrumbs.

**2** Heat the milk in a large saucepan. Add the remaining butter, the flour and cayenne, with the mustard powder. Bring to the boil over a low heat, whisking steadily until the mixture thickens to a smooth sauce.

**5** Add a few spoonfuls of the beaten egg whites to the sauce to lighten it. Beat well, then tip the rest of the whites into the pan and, with a large metal spoon, gently fold in the egg whites, using a figure-of-eight movement to combine the mixtures.

COOK'S TIP: It is important to serve soufflés the moment they are cooked and taken from the oven. Otherwise, the wonderful puffed top may sink.

**6** Pour the mixture into the prepared soufflé dish, level the top and, to help the soufflé rise evenly, run your finger around the inside rim of the dish. Place on a baking sheet. Sprinkle the remaining Parmesan over the top of the mixture and bake for about 25 minutes until risen and golden brown. Serve immediately.

VARIATIONS: This soufflé can also be served as a main meal by adding extra ingredients. Try putting a layer of lightly cooked (but not too moist) vegetables, such as ratatouille or sautéed mushrooms, at the bottom of the dish before adding the cheese mixture. Bake as above.

# Baked Herb Crêpes

These light herb pancakes, a regional speciality of France, are filled with spinach, cheese and pine nuts and served with a delicious tomato sauce.

Serves 4

INGREDIENTS
25 g/1 oz/½ cup chopped fresh herbs
15 ml/1 tbsp sunflower oil, plus extra
   for frying
120 ml/4 fl oz/½ cup milk
3 eggs
25 g/1 oz/¼ cup plain flour
pinch of salt

FOR THE SAUCE
30 ml/2 tbsp olive oil
1 small onion, chopped
2 garlic cloves, crushed
400 g/14 oz can chopped tomatoes
pinch of soft light brown sugar

FOR THE FILLING
450 g/1 lb fresh spinach
175 g/6 oz soft goat's cheese
25 g/1 oz/¼ cup pine nuts, toasted
5 sun-dried tomato halves in olive oil,
   drained and chopped
30 ml/2 tbsp shredded fresh basil
4 egg whites
oil, for greasing
salt, freshly grated nutmeg and freshly
   ground black pepper

**1** To make the crêpes, place the herbs and oil in a food processor and blend until smooth. Add the milk, eggs, flour and a pinch of salt and process again until smooth. Leave to rest for 30 minutes.

**2** Heat a small, non-stick frying pan and add a very small amount of oil. Pour out any excess oil and pour in a ladleful of the batter. Swirl around to cover the base. Cook for 2 minutes, turn over and cook for a further 1–2 minutes. Make seven more crêpes in the same way.

**3** To make the sauce, heat the oil in a small pan, add the onion and garlic and cook gently for 5 minutes. Add the tomatoes and sugar and cook for about 10 minutes until thickened. Purée in a blender, then sieve and set aside.

**4** To make the filling, clean, cook and drain the spinach then mix it with the cheese, pine nuts, sun-dried tomatoes and basil. Add salt, nutmeg and pepper.

**5** Preheat the oven to 190°C/375°F/ Gas 5. Whisk the egg whites until stiff. Fold one-third into the spinach mixture, then gently fold in the rest.

**6** Place one crêpe at a time on a lightly oiled baking sheet, add a tablespoonful of filling and fold into quarters. Bake for 12 minutes until set. Reheat the sauce and serve with the crêpes. If you want to prepare this in advance, cook the pancakes and sauce, and prepare the filling, but do not assemble until the last minute.

# Onion Tart

A classic tart from Alsace in eastern France. Traditionally served in small slices as a first course, it also makes a delicious main course.

Serves 4–6

INGREDIENTS
175 g/6 oz/1½ cups plain flour
75 g/3 oz/6 tbsp butter or half butter and
   half lard, chilled
30–45 ml/2–3 tbsp iced water

FOR THE FILLING
50 g/2 oz/¼ cup butter
900 g/2 lb Spanish onions,
   thinly sliced
1 egg plus 2 egg yolks
250 ml/8 fl oz/1 cup
   double cream
2.5 ml/½ tsp freshly grated nutmeg
salt and freshly ground
   black pepper

**1** Process the flour, a pinch of salt and the chilled butter or butter and lard in a food processor until reduced to fine crumbs. Add the iced water and process briefly to form a dough. Gather into a ball and chill for 40 minutes. Alternatively it can be done by hand.

**2** Meanwhile, to make the filling, melt the butter in a large saucepan and add the onions and a pinch of salt. Turn them in the butter. Cover and cook very gently, stirring frequently, for 30–40 minutes. The onions should gradually turn golden yellow.

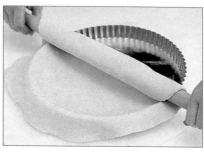

**3** Preheat the oven to 190°C/375°F/ Gas 5. Roll out the dough thinly and use to line a 23–25 cm/9–10 in loose-based flan tin. Line with foil, then bake for 10 minutes. Remove the foil and bake for another 4–5 minutes, until the pastry is lightly cooked to a pale brown. Reduce the oven temperature to 180°C/350°F/Gas 4.

**4** Beat the egg, egg yolks and cream together. Season with salt, lots of freshly ground black pepper and the grated nutmeg. Place half the onions in the pastry shell and add half the egg mixture. Add the remaining onions, then pour in as much of the custard as you can.

**5** Place on a baking sheet and bake on the middle shelf of the oven for 40–50 minutes or until the custard is risen, browned and set in the centre. Serve warm rather than piping hot.

VARIATIONS: There are many variations on this classic tart. Try adding 115 g/4 oz/¾ cup chopped sautéed lardons, or chopped fresh herbs. Use leeks and cook them for about 20 minutes in the butter to make flamiche, a classic Flemish tart.

47

# Omelette with Herbs

Omelettes are often served as a starter or supper dish in France and *fines herbes* combined with tangy, delicately soured cream make a perfect filling.

Serves 1

INGREDIENTS
2 eggs
15 g/½ oz/1 tbsp butter
15 ml/1 tbsp crème fraîche or soured cream
5 ml/1 tsp chopped fresh mixed herbs (such
   as tarragon, chives, parsley or marjoram)
salt and freshly ground black pepper

**1** Beat together the eggs and salt and pepper until well mixed. Melt the butter in an omelette pan or small, non-stick frying pan over a medium-high heat until foamy and light nutty brown, then pour in the eggs.

**2** As the egg mixture starts to set, lift up the sides using a fork or palette knife and tilt the pan to allow the uncooked eggs to run underneath.

**3** When the egg is too set to run but still soft, spoon the crème fraîche or soured cream down the centre and sprinkle with the herbs.

**4** To serve the omelette, hold the pan over a warmed plate. With a fork or palette knife, lift one edge of the omelette and fold it over the middle. Tilt the pan to help the omelette fold over on itself and slide it on to the plate.

# Ratatouille

This is a classic mix of vegetables that grow in the south of France.

Serves 6

INGREDIENTS

2 medium aubergines, about 450 g/1 lb
   total weight
60–75 ml/4–5 tbsp olive oil
1 large onion, sliced
2–3 garlic cloves, very finely chopped
1 large red or yellow pepper, seeded and cut
   into thin strips
2 large courgettes, cut into 1 cm/½ in slices
675g/1½ lb ripe tomatoes, peeled, seeded
   and chopped, or 400 g/14 oz can
   chopped tomatoes
5 ml/1 tsp dried herbes de Provence
salt and freshly ground black pepper

**1** Preheat the grill. Cut the aubergine into 2 cm/¾ in slices, brush with oil on both sides and grill until lightly browned, turning once. Cut into cubes.

**2** Heat 15 ml/1 tbsp of the oil in a large, heavy-based saucepan or flameproof casserole and cook the onion over a medium-low heat for about 10 minutes until lightly golden, stirring frequently. Add the garlic, red or yellow pepper and courgettes and cook for a further 10 minutes, stirring from time to time.

**3** Add the tomatoes and aubergine cubes, herbs and salt and pepper. Simmer gently, covered, over a low heat for about 20 minutes, stirring the mixture occasionally.

**4** Uncover and continue cooking for a further 20–25 minutes until all the vegetables are tender and the cooking liquid has thickened slightly. Serve hot or at room temperature.

# Potatoes Dauphinoise

These creamy potatoes are delicious with just about everything, but in France they are nearly always served with grilled or roast meat.

Serves 6

INGREDIENTS
1 kg/2¼ lb potatoes
900 ml/1½ pints/3¾ cups whole milk
freshly grated nutmeg
1 bay leaf
15–30 ml/1–2 tbsp butter, softened
2–3 garlic cloves, very finely chopped
45–60 ml/3–4 tbsp crème fraîche or
    whipping cream (optional)
salt and freshly ground black pepper

**1** Preheat the oven to 180°C/350°F/ Gas 4. Cut the potatoes into fairly thin slices and place in a large saucepan. Pour over the milk, adding more to cover if needed, and add salt and freshly ground black pepper, the nutmeg and bay leaf.

**2** Bring slowly to the boil over a medium heat and simmer for about 10 minutes until the potatoes just start to soften, but are not completely cooked, and the milk has thickened.

**3** Generously butter a 35 cm/14 in oval gratin dish or a 2 litre/3½ pint/ 8 cup shallow baking dish. Sprinkle the finely chopped garlic generously over the base of the dish, spreading it evenly.

**4** Using a slotted spoon, transfer the potatoes to the gratin or baking dish. Taste the milk and adjust the seasoning, then pour over enough of the milk to come just to the surface of the potatoes, but not cover them. Spoon a thin layer of crème fraîche or cream over the top, or, if you prefer, add more of the thickened milk to cover the potatoes.

**5** Bake the potatoes for about 1 hour until the milk is absorbed and the top is a deep golden brown. Serve hot.

COOK'S TIP: If cooked ahead, this dish will keep hot in a low oven for an hour or so, if necessary, without suffering; moisten the top with a little extra cream, if you like.

# Peas with Lettuce & Onion

Cooking them *à la Française* gives peas extra interest.

Serves 4–6

INGREDIENTS

15 g/½ oz/1 tbsp butter
1 small onion, finely chopped
1 small round lettuce
450 g/1 lb/3½ cups shelled fresh peas (from
   about 1.5 kg/3½ lb peas), or thawed
   frozen peas
45 ml/3 tbsp water
salt and freshly ground black pepper

**1** Melt the butter in a heavy-based saucepan. Add the onion and cook over a medium-low heat for about 3 minutes until just softened.

**2** Cut the lettuce in half through the core, then place cut side down on a board and slice into thin strips. Place the lettuce strips on top of the onion and add the peas and water. Season lightly with salt and pepper.

**3** Cover the pan tightly and cook the lettuce and peas over a low heat until the peas are tender – fresh peas will take 10–20 minutes, frozen peas about 10 minutes. Serve hot.

COOK'S TIP: Choose frozen petits pois as these have the best flavour.

# French Beans with Bacon & Cream

Beans are special when cooked in the French way with a creamy sauce.

Serves 4

INGREDIENTS

350 g/12 oz French beans
50–75 g/2–3 oz bacon, chopped
25 g/1 oz/2 tbsp butter or margarine
15 ml/1 tbsp plain flour
350 ml/12 fl oz/1½ cups milk and single
  cream, mixed
salt and freshly ground black pepper

**1** Preheat the oven to 190°C/375°F/ Gas 5. Trim the beans and cook in lightly salted boiling water for about 5 minutes until just tender. Drain them and place in an ovenproof dish.

**2** In a heavy-based pan, dry-fry the chopped bacon until crisp, crumble into very small pieces and stir into the beans.

**3** Melt the butter or margarine in a saucepan, and stir in the flour until well blended. Then slowly add the milk and cream to make a smooth sauce, stirring constantly. Season well with salt and pepper.

**4** Pour the sauce over the beans and carefully mix it in. Cover lightly with a piece of foil and bake in the oven for 15–20 minutes until hot.

# Mixed Green Salad

*Mesclun* is a Provençal salad composed of several kinds of leaves and herbs.

Serves 4–6

INGREDIENTS
200–225 g/7–8 oz mixed salad leaves
   (such as rocket, radicchio, lamb's lettuce
   and curly endive) and herbs
   (such as chervil, basil, parsley
   and tarragon)
1 garlic clove, peeled
30 ml/2 tbsp red wine or sherry vinegar
5 ml/1 tsp Dijon mustard (optional)
75–120 ml/5–8 tbsp extra virgin
   olive oil
salt and freshly ground
   black pepper

**1** Wash and spin dry the salad leaves and herbs. Rub a large salad bowl with the garlic clove and leave in the bowl.

**2** Add the vinegar, salt and pepper, and the mustard, if using. Stir to mix the ingredients and dissolve the salt, then slowly whisk in the oil.

**3** Remove the garlic clove and stir the vinaigrette to combine. Add the salad leaves and herbs to the bowl and toss well. Serve at once.

*Right: Mixed Green Salad (top);*
*Apple & Celeriac Salad*

# Apple & Celeriac Salad

Celeriac, despite its coarse appearance, has a unique sweet and subtle flavour.

Serves 3–4

INGREDIENTS
1 celeriac, about 450 g/1 lb, peeled
10–15 ml/2–3 tsp lemon juice
5 ml/1 tsp walnut oil (optional)
1 apple, preferably with
   a red skin
45 ml/3 tbsp mayonnaise
10 ml/2 tsp Dijon mustard
15 ml/1 tbsp finely chopped
   fresh parsley
salt and freshly ground black pepper

**1** Using a food processor or coarse cheese grater, shred the celeriac. Alternatively, cut it into very thin julienne strips. Place the celeriac in a bowl and sprinkle with the lemon juice and the walnut oil, if using. Stir well to mix.

**2** Peel the apple, if you like, cut into quarters and remove the core. Slice thinly crossways and toss gently with the celeriac.

**3** Mix together the mayonnaise, mustard, parsley and salt and pepper to taste. Stir into the celeriac mixture and mix well. Chill for several hours until ready to serve.

# Tarte Tatin

This scrumptious French "upside-down" apple tart is very easy to make.

Serves 6–8

INGREDIENTS
3 Braeburn, Cox's Orange Pippin,
    Granny Smith or firm
    dessert apples
juice of ½ lemon
50 g/2 oz/¼ cup butter, softened
75 g/3 oz/scant ½ cup caster sugar
250 g/9 oz ready-rolled
    puff pastry
single cream, to serve

1 Preheat the oven to 220°C/425°F/
Gas 7. Cut the apples in quarters and
remove the cores. Toss the apple
quarters in the lemon juice to prevent
them discolouring.

2 Spread the butter over the base of a
20 cm/8 in heavy-based omelette pan
that can safely be used in the oven.
Sprinkle the caster sugar over the
butter and add the apple wedges,
rounded side down.

3 Cook over a medium heat for
15–20 minutes or until the apples
are golden.

4 Cut the pastry into a 25 cm/10 in
round, place on top of the apples and
tuck the edges in with a knife. Place
the pan in the oven and bake for
15–20 minutes or until the pastry is
golden. Carefully invert the tart on to a
plate. Cool slightly and serve with cream.

# Crêpes Suzette with Cointreau

A classic French dessert of flambéed pancakes filled with flavoured butter.

Serves 6

INGREDIENTS
175 g/6 oz/¾ cup unsalted butter
50 g/2 oz/¼ cup granulated sugar
grated rind of 2 oranges
30 ml/2 tbsp Cointreau
115 g/4 oz/1 cup plain flour
2.5 ml/½ tsp salt
2 eggs, beaten
300 ml/½ pint/1¼ cups milk
oil, for frying
juice of 2 oranges
45 ml/3 tbsp Cognac
icing sugar, for dusting
strips of thinly pared orange rind,
    to decorate

**1** To make the orange butter, cream the butter with the sugar. Stir in the orange rind and Cointreau. Set aside.

**2** Sift the flour and salt into a bowl, make a well in the centre and add the eggs. Mix thoroughly. Gradually stir in the milk and beat to a smooth batter.

**3** Heat the oil in a frying pan and pour in batter to make a thin 15 cm/6 in pancake. Cook until the underside is golden, turn and cook the other side. Slide out of the pan. Make five more. Spread with half the butter, fold into quarters.

**4** Heat the rest of the orange butter in the pan with the orange juice, add the pancakes and turn to heat through. Push to one side of the pan and pour in the Cognac. Heat, then carefully set alight. When the flames die down, spoon the sauce over the pancakes. Serve dusted with icing sugar and decorated with orange rind.

# Coffee Cream Profiteroles

Enjoy a taste of France with these crisp-textured coffee choux pastry puffs, filled with cream and drizzled with a white chocolate sauce.

Serves 6

INGREDIENTS
65 g/2½ oz/generous ½ cup plain
    white flour
pinch of salt
50 g/2 oz/¼ cup butter
150 ml/¼ pint/⅔ cup brewed coffee
2 eggs, lightly beaten
250 ml/8 fl oz/1 cup
    double cream

FOR THE WHITE CHOCOLATE SAUCE
50 g/2 oz/¼ cup sugar
100 ml/3½ fl oz/scant ½ cup water
150 g/5 oz good-quality white dessert
    chocolate, broken into pieces
25 g/1 oz/2 tbsp unsalted butter
45 ml/3 tbsp double cream
30 ml/2 tbsp coffee liqueur, such as Tia
    Maria, Kahlúa or Toussaint

**1** Preheat the oven to 220°C/425°F/ Gas 7. Sift the flour and salt on to a piece of greaseproof paper. Cut the butter into pieces and put in a pan with the coffee.

**2** Bring to a rolling boil, then remove from the heat and tip in all the flour. Beat until the mixture is thick and smooth and leaves the sides of the pan. Leave to cool for 2 minutes.

**3** Gradually add the eggs, beating well between each addition. Spoon the mixture into a piping bag fitted with a 1 cm/½ in plain nozzle.

**4** Pipe about 24 small buns on to a dampened baking sheet. Bake for 20 minutes, until well risen and crisp. Remove the buns from the oven and pierce the side of each one with a sharp knife to let out the steam.

**5** To make the sauce, put the sugar and water in a heavy-based pan and heat gently until dissolved. Bring to the boil and simmer for 3 minutes. Remove from the heat. Add the chocolate and butter, stirring until smooth. Stir in the cream and liqueur.

**6** To assemble, whip the cream until soft peaks form. Using a piping bag, fill the choux buns through the slits in the sides. Arrange on plates and pour a little of the sauce over. Serve the remaining sauce separately.

# Black Cherry Clafoutis

Another great French invention, best made using slightly tart black cherries, and originally served at harvest time.

Serves 6

INGREDIENTS

25 g/1 oz/2 tbsp butter, for greasing
450 g/1 lb/2 cups black cherries, stoned
25 g/1 oz/¼ cup plain flour
50 g/2 oz/½ cup icing sugar, plus
   extra for dusting
4 eggs, beaten
250 ml/8 fl oz/1 cup creamy milk
30 ml/2 tbsp Kirsch (cherry liqueur)

1  Preheat the oven to 180°C/350°F/ Gas 4. Use the butter to thickly grease a 1.2 litre/2 pint/5 cup gratin dish. Scatter the cherries over the base.

2  Sift the flour and icing sugar together into a large mixing bowl and gradually whisk in the eggs until the mixture is smooth. Slowly whisk in the milk until well blended, then stir in the Kirsch.

3  Pour the batter carefully over the cherries in the gratin dish. Then bake for 35–45 minutes or until just set and lightly golden.

4  Remove the pudding from the oven and allow to cool for about 15 minutes. Dust liberally with icing sugar just before serving.

# Framboise Sabayon with Blueberries & Raspberries

Using framboise, a French raspberry liqueur, this couldn't be simpler to prepare and tastes superb.

Serves 4

INGREDIENTS
115 g/4 oz/1 cup fresh blueberries
175 g/6 oz/1 cup fresh raspberries
3 egg yolks
60 ml/4 tbsp framboise (raspberry liqueur)
25 g/1 oz/2 tbsp caster sugar, plus extra
 for topping

VARIATION: In the winter, when fresh soft fruits are out of season (and expensive), try this with dried apricots macerated in brandy and topped with crème fraîche.

**1** Arrange the fresh blueberries and raspberries in wide flameproof soup bowls or on flameproof dessert plates.

**2** Mix the egg yolks, framboise (raspberry liqueur) and sugar in a large heatproof bowl. Place the bowl over a pan of barely simmering water and whisk until the mixture is thick and foamy. Preheat the grill.

**3** Spoon the sauce over the fruits, sprinkle with a little sugar and flash briefly under the hot grill until the sugar caramelizes and turns golden. Serve immediately.

# Bitter Chocolate Mousse

This rich and extremely delicious mousse is the quintessential French dessert. Use the darkest chocolate you can find to achieve the most intense bitter chocolate flavour.

Serves 8

INGREDIENTS
225 g/8 oz plain 70% chocolate, chopped
60 ml/4 tbsp water
30 ml/2 tbsp orange liqueur
  or brandy
30 g/1 oz/2 tbsp unsalted butter, cut into
  small pieces
4 eggs, separated
90 ml/6 tbsp whipping cream
1.5 ml/¼ tsp cream of tartar
45 ml/3 tbsp caster sugar
crème fraîche or soured cream and chocolate
  curls, to serve (optional)

**1** Place the chocolate and water in a heavy-based saucepan. Melt over a very low heat, stirring. Remove the pan from the heat and whisk in the liqueur or brandy and butter. Beat the egg yolks for about 3 minutes until thick and creamy, then slowly beat into the melted chocolate until well blended. Set aside.

**2** Whip the cream until soft peaks form and stir a spoonful into the chocolate mixture to lighten it. Fold in the remaining cream.

**3** In a clean, grease-free bowl, use an electric mixer to slowly beat the egg whites until frothy. Add the cream of tartar, increase the speed and continue beating until the egg whites form soft peaks. Gradually sprinkle the sugar over and continue beating until the whites are stiff and glossy.

**4** Using a rubber spatula or large metal spoon, stir a quarter of the egg whites into the chocolate mixture using a gentle figure-of-eight motion.

**5** Gently fold in the remaining whites, cutting down to the bottom, along the sides and up to the top in a semicircular motion until they are just combined. Don't worry about a few white streaks.

**6** Carefully spoon into a 2 litre/ 3½ pint/8 cup dish or into eight individual dishes. Chill for at least 2 hours until firmly set.

**7** Spoon a little crème fraîche or soured cream over the mousse and decorate with chocolate curls, if you wish, before serving.

# This edition is published by Southwater

Southwater is an imprint of
Anness Publishing Ltd
Hermes House
88–89 Blackfriars Road
London SE1 8HA
tel. 020 7401 2077
fax 020 7633 9499

Distributed in the USA by
Anness Publishing Inc.
27 West 20th Street
Suite 504
New York
NY 10011
fax 212 807 6813

Distributed in the UK by
The Manning Partnership
251–253 London Road East
Batheaston
Bath BA1 7RL
tel. 01225 852 727
fax 01225 852 852

Distributed in Australia by
Sandstone Publishing
Unit 1, 360 Norton Street, Leichhardt
New South Wales 2040
tel. 02 9560 7888
fax 02 9560 7488

Publisher: Joanna Lorenz
Managing Editor: Helen Sudell
Editor: Valerie Ferguson
Series Designer: Bobbie Colgate Stone
Designer: Andrew Heath
Production Controller: Joanna King

Recipes contributed by: Catherine Atkinson,
Alex Barker, Jacqueline Clark, Carole Clements,
Nicola Diggins, Brian Glover, Christine Ingram,
Lucy Knox, Sally Mansfield, Maggie Mayhew,
Norma Miller, Keith Richmond,
Elizabeth Wolf-Cohen

Photography: Louise Dare, James Duncan,
Michelle Garrett, Amanda Heywood,
Janine Hosegood, David Jordan,
William Lingwood, Patrick McLeavey, Steve Moss,
Craig Robertson, Sam Stowell

Notes:
For all recipes, quantities are given in both metric and imperial measures and, where appropriate, measures are also given in standard cups and spoons.
Follow one set, but not a mixture, because they are not interchangeable.

Standard spoon and cup measures are level.

1 tsp = 5 ml    1 tbsp = 15 ml

1 cup = 250 ml/8 fl oz

Australian standard tablespoons are 20 ml. Australian readers should use 3 tsp in place of 1 tbsp for measuring small quantities of gelatine, cornflour, salt, etc.

Medium eggs are used unless otherwise stated.

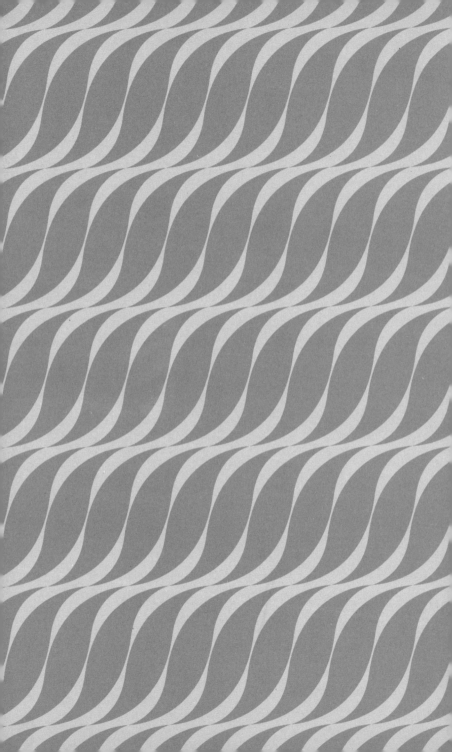